Teasing the Grace

poems and stories

Sharon J. Sanders

authorHOUSE®

AuthorHouse™
1663 Liberty Drive
Bloomington, IN 47403
www.authorhouse.com
Phone: 1-800-839-8640

First published by AuthorHouse   10/18/2010

ISBN: 978-1-4520-8915-7 (sc)
ISBN: 978-1-4520-8916-4 (e)

Library of Congress Control Number: 2010915703

Printed in the United States of America

This book is printed on acid-free paper.

Certain stock imagery © Thinkstock.

To Martha

my lovely distraction

A performer cannot be an attraction while suffering from distraction, unless that distraction is recognized as a greater attraction, treated as such and somehow brought into the arena.

--Pierre Delattre

Contents

A Ritual for the Chaos

you are the poem I want to ingest

you are absolutely complete and perfect

yet growing

together we will examine the words, the gestures,

the tones, the structure

that are you

together we will experience a performance

that is you

together we will learn how to see you growing

and then together we will hear the song

of you shaping you, testing rhythms

till you find the ones that make

your DNA hum true as it spirals

through the chaos.

let this be a ritual for the chaos.

Against All Orders

It is war.

In spite of the commands

to hold and wait

my hands twitch to touch

you my tongue

pushes against my

teeth wanting out

to caress your flesh.

My legs flex around your

shadow and would draw you

into them if they could.

As I clamp shut the jaw,

cross the legs with hands

between

I know it is war.

The tail wags

the heart pounds

and saliva escapes the lips.

It is war

and the body is winning.

As I See Myself Changing

A monologue for a woman aged 40-60.

Setting is a platform with a stationary bicycle and a chair or chair-height cube on it.

A WOMAN comes out walking wearily, eyes down. She is dressed in dowdy exercise clothes. On stepping up to the platform, she raises her eyes to the audience—suddenly straightens up, smoothes her hair, shirt, pauses, then dismisses the effort and continues wearily to the stationary bicycle, climbs on, wipes sweat off her brow and begins to pedal with no energy, eyes down. 15 seconds pass….she glances at the audience, stops pedaling, glares at someone in the audience.
Don't you know it's rude to stare? *(She pedals 2 or 3 more turns and grumbles to herself)* You're not going anywhere, either. *(pause).*

A body starts to lose muscle mass—maybe you don't know that. Young people are so smug—they don't think about getting older. Then, about the time you start to lose muscle mass—they don't tell you this either—you start to lose the energy to do anything about it. You never know when your knees are going to buckle or when your whole body's going to turn to tortured pudding… And just about the time you think you'll get on this thing and save a little muscle mass, here comes a hot flash and all the pudding inside you just goes to a boil and you got steam coming out of your eyebrows…and you got to go lie down. *(Stops pedaling, glares at the audience.)* Are you smirking? *(shouting)* Hot Flashes! Change of Life! Menopause! Smirk, smirk, smirk! Let me give you one piece of advice: Don't smirk at a menopausal woman! We can get pretty testy. *(She pauses, gets off the bicycle and sits on the chair/cube or edge of platform.)*

Nobody really wants to talk about it—or even think about it. When this stuff started happening with me, I wanted to talk to some older women to find out more—what did you feel? How long did it go on? What did it mean to you? So, I'm sitting at the breakfast table with my mother and sister and I ask, "What was menopause like for you?" My sister *smirk*s and reminds me that she had a hysterectomy when she was 38, as if that were very clever of her. My mother swallows a hem and a hah and says well, she seems to remember that her legs ached. Thank you very much! So much for family wisdom.

So, back on my own. What *does* it mean? Will I really mind when the bleeding stops? No more pads, tampons, or double pads because tampons may not be safe? No more wearing dark clothing because I might leak. No more running off to the bathroom because I feel wet and don't know if it's sex or blood, and then walking around with a wad of stiff, commercial toilet paper stuffed between my legs. I *will* be glad to say goodbye to all that.

My periods started when I was 12. I discovered the light-brown stains when I woke and I went to school in a daze. After school, I took my solid chocolate

Easter bunny and went to the movies. I sat in the dark theater crying and eating chocolate and knowing that the good life was over. I *knew* this was God's special punishment for my decision not to be a missionary to Africa—a decision I had made just recently and after much soul-searching.

I had friends whose mothers celebrated their first periods. Nobody celebrated my becoming a woman. I held a funeral there alone in the dark theater while Susan Hayward and Charlton Heston agonized on the screen.

I grew a little bit wiser and more accepting as time went by, but I never liked my periods, and there's a 12 year-old who likes to point out to me that if the punishment is being lifted now, it's a bit late. Right! The curse is lifted, and I look in the mirror at a woman who is growing old. Thank you very much!

Our culture says that menopause signals loss—loss of youth, vitality, juices, the ability to have babies, to attract love—and lately I have been feeling that loss. I made a conscious decision not have children and I don't truly regret it, but one day when the hot flashes were too much for me, I spent an hour in my gynecologist's waiting room with a mother and her newborn. As I watched that mother stare at her baby and touch its cheek with her finger, knowing she was looking at the proof that her blood had not been wasted but had been transformed into this living creature of charm and potential, I felt the loss, the sadness, the envy that was buried so deeply in me.

I am changing, and the changing is painful. I am losing muscle, energy, my memory is less and less dependable, my faith in a certain kind of control is fading, and I have fears—fears that there will be nothing of value to replace what is lost.

But, there are moments, coming to me stronger and staying with me longer, when I see that this painful, dark passage may be a transition. As I lie in my bed and watch the moon rise, remembering how I used to feel proud that my bleeding responded to the pull of the moon, I realize that although I am not bleeding, I *am* feeling the pull of the moon in all of my body. I hear Marge Piercy say "the moon is always female," and I suddenly know that I have not lost anything. For almost 40 years I have just been in training with the moon as my teacher. Each month, for four or five days, I was given lessons in letting go, in feeling intensely, in tapping my deepest self, in learning to find the still place in which I could hear my heart speak. *(pause)* Is it possible that I am about to graduate? About to come into my fullness as a woman? Is it possible that I am moving into full-time awareness that life is an incredible flow of illusion created for our pleasure and enlightenment? Is it possible that all I am being asked to do is to sit still and reflect the light? Is it possible that I am becoming partners with the moon?

As I grow older, I hear the ocean inside me, and, like the ocean, I am sometimes turbulent and sometimes peaceful, but always powerful, emotional and self-contained; always related to the shore; and always responsive to the moon.

So, maybe, just maybe, the meaning of menopause is the stopping of the monthlies and the beginning of the always. Maybe we are being called to let ourselves grow softer, to sit in hot tubs and make time for naps. Maybe it is time to celebrate the going of the memory. Maybe not remembering how something was will allow us to see how it is without fear or boredom. A change of life, a new life.

I'm going to try to let it happen, to feel the changing and the changes. *(She pauses and returns to the bicycle.)*

I want to suggest that if you get yourself one of these things, don't be too hard on yourself if you don't use it because maybe this is not a time for doing—just for being—being a woman growing older. As for me, I'm going to let the moon pull on me more and more. I want to see what's going to come.

Bad Girl

I don't know when it started

Perhaps when one of us was killed

for no other reason

than hatred of our difference

hatred of our power to create love and life

and her daughter watching

unable to assimilate

unable to wrap her mind around

that kind of hatred

took it to mean that

she was bad

--bad girl—bad girl—die—bad girl—

and quietly crept away

to hide from the hatred that could

and would—bad girl—kill—

bad girl—she said to her daughter

my great-great-great-grandmother

the one whose body flowed

through the world like trees in breeze

--bad girl—cover your breasts

don't smile at strangers

don't even look—bad girl—

lower your eyes

stay home and hate yourself

teach your daughter well

or they will kill her—bad girl—

bad girl—hate yourself or

they will kill you

teach your daughter well

to survive—bad girl

Cleveland in Gray Winter

(or *Cleveland Almost Anytime*)

White-headed ladies trundle past artichokes and peppers red as the heart of hell

Thumb-devouring children and pocketed men snuggle in to the game of "I wanna go home"

While musky dark-nailed men shout "Lady! Want a potted flower? want tomatoes,

Lady

Want, want, want?"

And always I answer with a quick nod No and a look of apology for denying their fruit, their soil.

Walk through Cleveland—over bridges under trestles down steep crusted banks to railroad tracks bordering a brown industrial river

Past square brick monsters of people-cubicled glass and steel swing homes of children screaming their unvoiced desire to be as much at least as a tomato with a stall of its own, as much as a loaf of

Real Jewish rye admired in its uncut whole (better than a teddy bear)

A house hovering on a chasm yet firm beyond cabbages and shopping bags and white-trousered parking attendants who look and lust and wave the next car into the system of

Buy, sell, go home, raise fruit and vegetable, rise to do it all again—

Lady, want to buy, lady want?

Eyes see customer no longer see red heart of hell for sale of plumbing plums of Eden bruised by eyes of color-blind bargainers.

Whistle of train—the track rumbling five hundred yards ahead of its mover announcing screaming—

Lady—want?

Then pocket money—buy no red hearts but hamburger coffee a pair of socks to put on in the store and walk out feeling

Vagrant feeling less than these gray women with bags and hats and ankle coats and stubby black shoes to level out the sullen earth

The sky—upturned blue sprung from—

the pure unchanging

Blue cupping madness saying never mind—no fear

Perfect of loaves and solid of cabbages mere reminders of

The angels are white—someone

put petunias around St. Francis the same someone

put iron bars around the petunias unadorned

Unadorned the sky—the sky with one streak of white my feet

Fly over bridges, under trestles—a girder shoots up

from unseen

River and leaps crooked at the sky lunging my feet
with it and

Laughing doors open—windows

Expand in chuckles.

The Ballad of the Twin Towers

Early that day she left our bed

> For work across the bay.

"Stay awhile, my love, my dear.

> Stay awhile and play."

"You know I can't. I have to go.

> Work's what pays our way,

Though the bed is warm and I would love

> To stay awhile and play."

"Well, go then, love, for the sooner you go,

> The sooner you come back today.

I'll clean the house; I'll wash the clothes,

> And later we will play."

"I'll kiss you now before I go.

> I'll miss you all the day.

I'll call you soon when I'm at work,

> And on the phone we'll play."

She left me then, all smiles and sweet—

Took the ferry across the bay.

I wished her well, "Be careful, dear.

Hurry back to me. We'll play"

What happened next, I cannot say.

Like any other day—

She safe at work and I at home,

Hearts stretched across the bay.

Where she was when the towers fell—

A moment in a day—

Where she was no one can tell,

But she didn't call to play.

The rubble's all taken off the streets;

The ash has blown away.

But you, my dear, never came back

To stay awhile and play.

Before I Was Afraid

Before I was afraid
I walked to school each day
and if the train was stopped
blocking my way
I simply climbed over it
and went on to my day.

Before I was afraid
I climbed tall trees
trusting that each limb
if tested with half my weight
would hold all my weight
and they did.

Before I was afraid
I believed that if I held the rope tight
and flung myself from the tallest limb
it would take me safely
across the gully
and deliver me into the soft woods

and it did.

Before I was afraid
I went to my neighbor's doors often
confident that they would want
to buy my blackberries and goldfish
confident that they would have
some small job to pay me for
and they did.

Before I was afraid
I rode my bike into the
lonely country up dirt roads
delivering papers while hounds
barked and snapped at the cards
flapping on my spokes
stopping in broken-down stores
of beans, bread, soda pop and salt licks
to visit with old sun-weathered men
in overalls knowing they welcomed
my interruption into their dreary timeless days
and they did.

Before I was afraid

healing was guaranteed

fatigue washed away in the night

cuts and bruises faded quickly in the long days.

Before I was afraid

tears were brief interruptions

in the joyous focus of the present

I knew they would stop

as soon as I could catch my breath

and they did.

Before I was afraid

I had such contempt for fear

such arrogance of me

until one night

walking home in the soft dark

from a friend's house

I heard footsteps behind me

and then in an instant the dark

hardened and split

I heard purpose in those steps.

and I raced that purpose

creating a tunnel in the dark and won

the safety of my home.

I am still trying to catch my breath

trying to remember what it was like

before I was afraid.

As It Should Be

"Give me a G

Give me an O

Give me a G O D

Who d'ya love?

Who d'ya love?

Me, me, me."

On the last words, god leaped into the air, did three backward somersaults, landed lightly but firmly in the two-footed stance, arms lifted high above his head, chin up triumphantly. He was proud of the landing— had designed it himself and was particularly gratified to see that all the little gymnasts on earth had adopted it and made every attempt to use it as he had intended.

Not like some of his inventions. God started to frown, but quickly he turned that frown upside down and put on a happy face which he lifted to the sky as he heard infinite echoes of "me, me, me" throughout heaven. As it should be.

If only it were all that simple. God spent several moments pondering each problem that arose, knowing that a creative response would come. God was very creative—it was the core of his nature. Ideas would pop into his head with no apparent effort, and he would transfer them to the appropriate host as easily as thinking them. As it should be.

So far, only the gymnasts and circus performers seemed to get it consistently right. Only they took his ideas and formed them into meaningful ritual. He loved to watch them. Everything they did was right, or close to it, except the animal acts. He had never intended animals to be used the way they were used in the circus. But high marks to the balance beam and his magnificat—the tightrope. To the parallel bars, the trapeze in flight against gravity, the uneven bars, the rings. He approved heartily of the clowns with all their jokes about themselves. When he saw what Cirque de Soleil had done with his ideas, he thought he had gone to heaven. As it should be.

He never knew what earthlings might do with his ideas. Every single thought he sent out was caught by at least one of them. Sometimes, the idea spread and developed into a jewel, like the circus. Sometimes, an idea caught the fancy of many earthlings at once, like the hula hoop. For a while there, it seemed that everyone on earth would learn to fly a perfect circle through the air with just the twists of their bodies. But they couldn't take it to the next level, and the hoops, one by one, lay dusty in attics and garages until they went to the landfill. So many of his ideas were lost this way. When the earthlings failed to develop them, they called them fads, saying the word with some contempt as if it were the fault of the ideas that they didn't transform into the full gift that they were. The mood ring and the pet rock were among some of his ideas that had failed in the hands of the earthlings. Perhaps they would come back and be realized. As it should be.

Ironically, one of his happiest ideas was one of his most abused ideas. The happy face, which he still used almost daily, had at first delighted people of all ages. They drew the simple happy face on notes and letters and children's creations, and began saying "Have a nice day" as standard parting words. It went from a fresh idea to a cloying cliché in record time. Then, it began to appear on pharmaceutical notepads. "Have a nice day"—Smiley face—"Take elavil."

But the worst abuse of the happy face occurred when a corporation, known for exploiting its workers, took the happy face, turned it into an animated logo, and used it to exploit the buying public by making them believe that the happy face "cut" prices for them. This corporation's demise was on god's short list. As it should be.

He thought fondly of some of his pet ideas. Peace and unconditional acceptance, though not enjoying widespread popularity, had persisted, kept alive by small groups and individuals throughout the span of human life. These ideas seemed to be waiting for enough momentum to push them into a form. Charles Schultz almost got it when he proposed that every child should be given a banjo at birth. But too many parents had already bought footballs and Barbie dolls.

God thought the critical moment was near. Just a few more bumper stickers might do it. Maybe a new cheer would spark the shift. Perhaps another Buddha or Jesus, Gandhi or Martin Luther King would make the difference. As it should be.

War was how the humans expressed their unwillingness to share, and wars were actually becoming less popular. There had been no protestors at the Crusades. No ordinary men and women standing in quiet vigil along the dusty road to Damascus, no chanting, no peace signs or draped flower garlands hung from swords. Most countries today actually had to pay people to fight, or promise them an immediate spot in heaven if they died fighting. They came to heaven all right, and god set them straight. He washed the blood off personally, gave them milk and cookies and sent them to peace cheerleading school. As it should be.

It was not god's job to create the new form. God was an idea, flinging sparks to those who would catch them and make fire. God was the word and the word was god. As it should be.

"Give me an 'H'

Give me an 'A'

Give me a 'P', 'P', 'Y'

Give me an 'F'

Give me an 'A'

Give me a 'C'

Give me an 'E'

Who d'ya love?

Who d'ya love?

Me, me, me

On the last words, god leaped into the air, did three backward somersaults, landed lightly but firmly in the two-footed stance, arms lifted high above his head, chin up triumphantly. As it should be.

Blue Mother, Water Friend

Blue mother,

Water friend,

floating

I am me

held by you.

I can raise

my feet, my head, my belly.

Filling with air

I can raise my whole body.

On your lap

I can dangle, stretch and breathe

slowly, simply

stroked and stroking.

You call me to enter,

to see the wonders

of your surround.

I pause and hesitate.

With only faith

to tell me I have form,

will I be me

held by you,
or will I be
Blue mother,
Water friend?

Cellular Talking

you now

with your long smooth

legs around me

duet of rhythms

coming in the night

and going in the morning

oiled

my skin

sings against yours

cellular talking

Clean These Juices

clean

these juices

are fresh for you

all new

these muscles

are tuned to you

relentless tonguing

mines your harvest

are you ripe for me?

Couldn't We Just?

Couldn't we just go ahead

and pretend that we've been lovers

pretend that we've already touched

and loved and given pleasure

 to the most private parts of each

other's bodies

pretend that we have had those

moments of abandon and are

lying breathless and careless

piled upon each other

like a litter of kittens

sweaty and imperfect

our breasts and buttocks hanging out?

Couldn't we just pretend

that we've shown the beast

and the beast has been declared

a beauty?

Couldn't we just pretend that we can look

in each other's eyes without the

hardness of fear

pretend that we can touch a nipple and

laugh when it rises up to meet us

pretend we could slide an arm around

a waist and feel the subtle yielding?

Couldn't we just pretend

that we won't hurt each other?

Couldn't we just?

In The Blank Spaces

Immobolize me, immortalize me

Hold me still on this moment

Tight, strained, trembling on possibility

With your joy before me

In an outstretched, untouched hand.

In the blank spaces between the black

      marks on the clock

Hold me still on this moment.

Somewhere Else

The door was open. She couldn't remember if she had opened it. What was worse, she couldn't remember if it should be open or shut. She sat on the edge of the bed and tried to puzzle it out. If the door is open, the dog can come in; if the door is closed, the cat can't go out. If the door is open, the cat can come in and the dog can go out. Where *was* the cat? Where was the dog? She couldn't see them anywhere in the room. Did that mean they were out, and where did she want them to be? Was there a previous decision about this door—one that would cover all possibilities, like a rule? She couldn't remember, but she desperately needed a rule to go by right now. Why? Well, because she seemed to be stuck right now. Why was she sitting on the bed with one foot in her pantyhose and one foot out? This question felt akin to the door question, which was... where is the cat? No, that's not it. The pantyhose are in her hands. One foot is on. The door is open. The cat is...somewhere else. That's it! Somewhere else. That thought seemed to resolve everything. She was somewhere else. That's why she couldn't know the rules. She wasn't where they were. She was somewhere else.

Forget the rules. The big question is where is she and does anyone know that she is not really here sitting on the edge of the bed with one foot in her pantyhose? She should get help. Someone should help her, but she is crying, great big silent tears. No one will come to help her. No one helps a crybaby. That sounded like a rule: no one helps a crybaby. But how could they when she is somewhere else?

She had to go away. Had to go away from him and the open door. If the door was open, he could come in, but she could go out. Was that the rule she was looking for?

She had to go where he wasn't. Had to be somewhere else. But then, where was she? And how would anyone be able to find her? Would they even see her or would they think she was sitting here on the edge of the bed with one foot in her pantyhose? No, they wouldn't. They'd just close the door and look somewhere else for her, but they'd never find her because she'd be here, then. It would always be somewhere else. He would chase her from room to room and he would always find her before anyone could help her or tell her if the door should be open or shut.

So much depended on the door, but the door depended on the rules, and the rules depended on someone else, and if he were that someone else, she was doomed to sit here on the edge of the bed with one foot in her pantyhose and tears soaking her nightgown.

Dead or Alive

Buzzards are okay.

I find them hard to love,

revolting from thoughts of them

when I am in the city,

preferring to think of dolphins and unicorns

in my dream-making time.

But when I am traveling,

driving through the scrub, farm and marsh lands

of Georgia, I am reminded that

buzzards are okay.

And those days, I declare

Buzzard Appreciation Day.

Strong, clean-lined, swift and lazy,

they never kill, preferring flight from danger

and carrion for food.

Truly they deserve the reputation of the dove—

perfect pacifists, perfect fruitarians of the flesh.

I would like to know that my body

someday might provide a feast for

my buzzard friends.

I would try to keep my flesh sweet for you.

You could begin with ten plump toes

for hors d'oevres and proceed

through the succulence of limbs and flanks and breasts.

If that, however, is too much for your

delicate sensibilities,

carry me out to the marshlands, gather around

me in a circle, and let the buzzards show you

how to finish with the body.

When they have picked off all the flesh and

my bones lie gleaming white in the

sun, I hope you will appreciate the

smile on my lipless face.

And, if that too, is more than you can

stomach, you romantic babes,

plant me in your garden.

Out of my head will spring giant sunflowers,

my limbs will give you squash, cucumber,

all manner of trailing things.

Out of my loins I will bring forth melons,

and out of my mouth will come

the odor of roses.

Early Morning Breeze

Early morning breeze

the sound of garbage trucks and birds

clothesline and rose arbor.

This window I sit behind

relieves me of choice,

cuts out one four-foot square

of the world

and frames for me a whole.

I should have been a painter,

but how in color would I show

the smoky rose of remembered night music?

the silver line that runs between my

hand and your body?

or the gold flecks in the black night of my dream?

How could I paint the amber scream

that rises to crystallize like ice membrane

and melts down to mix with soot?

It is so much simpler

behind my four-foot square of world.

Clothesline and rose arbor.

Eddie and Rain

when it's raining and the grass

is bare-toe squishy

the curled water gushes down

to the deepplace

catching in its tendrils

all the grasses from yesterday's mowing

washing them down in one great gulp

of little boy's delight

who splashes high

and squeals as the splashes

reach his face

and splashes again

higher

until the fervent dervishes of the sun

consume the glistening drops

of his baby passion

My Grandmother Died in Diapers

My grandmother died in diapers

calling out "this baby needs to be

changed." She spent her last days

wrapped in her soft loose flesh free

at last from muscle to

wash   iron   fetch   and carry

all those other babies she had tended

calling out for her own needs

and babbling with her four-year-old brother

seventy-two years dead.

       My mother changed her diapers

       held her hand and told the family

       "I'm afraid grandma is going senile"

       and held on to 1971.

       My mother knows more than she lets on.

Orphaned at twelve, my grandmother

was adopted into a motherless family

of eight younger children (dare I say "sold"?)

Her first husband died of tuberculosis

her second, an abusive alcoholic, was

divorced by a woman for whom

divorce was a palpable sin.

        My mother combed her hair

        let her help with the chores

        as long as she could stand

        and told the family

        "I don't know why she won't rest."

        My mother knows more than she lets on.

My grandmother carried two children and a

cow through the Depression, accepting

no charity from that Roosevelt man.

The children grown, she hired out

as a companion to the sick and dying.

When I was born, she was at home tending

my sister and waiting

to give me my name, the female name

that meant Jesus to her

Pentecostal mind.

        I had not expected to cry

        at the funeral. I traveled

        to Missouri to be with

        my mother, to hold

the line of mother daughter daughter

against the blow of death. When I saw

my grandmother's body without its life

without its caring movement, I wept alone.

My mother said to the family,

"Doesn't she look nice?"

and after the funeral, she wanted tacos.

My mother knows more than she lets on.

Empty in the Center

Suddenly the room was empty.

Silence crept in from the corners

where it had been hiding

and stretched its paws out

toward where she stood in the center.

The lights yawned and faded

as muscles went lax

where she stood in the center.

The walls breathed deeply in and out.

She closed her eyes

and slid into the emptiness.

For Your Gender's Sake
(a birth poem for Rachel)

May you never, for your gender's sake

    Hear the brother taunting brother with the

    words "girl-cunt-woman-bitch-sissy-sister."

May you never, for your gender's sake

    Hear the sister say

    "Don't act so smart; they won't like it."

May you never, for your gender's sake

    Hear the mother say

    "Be still. Be quiet. Act like a lady."

    May you never even consider acting like a lady

    except in a play and for a great deal of money.

May you never, for your gender's sake

    Hear the father say

    "You can catch more flies with honey than with salt."

May you never, for your gender's sake

    Be asked to shorten your shorts, lengthen

    your hair or reshape your nose, breasts or

    thighs for someone else's pleasure.

May you never, for your gender's sake

Be told your menstrual blood is unclean, your
voice too loud, your energy too high, your
dreams too big, your tears too shameful,
your words too rude.

May you never, for your gender's sake
Feel the rage of being assumed stupid,
helpless, hysterical or castrating.

May you never, for your gender's sake
Be given the phrase in praise
"You think like a man."

May you never, for your gender's sake
Be put on the marriage market or feel the
shame of not being put on the marriage market.

May you never, for your gender's sake
Question your right to walk on any street at
any time.

May you never, for your gender's sake
Experience your flesh violated, your soul
mocked,your mind denied.

May you never, for your gender's sake
Be wounded.

Friends

We pour ourselves into each other

    like water poured from one cup to another

    streaming a bridge of flashing water

    across the space

as I empty out, I fill you

full, you return into my emptiness

The bridge is charged with newly made energy

    as we empty that which is full

    and fill that which is empty.

From a Dream of the Growing Boat

This island is not my home

although it welcomes me

feeds me

holds me safe from the endless sea

while my boat grows larger

scraped and caulked

sails unfurled for repair.

This island is not my home.

Although it welcomes me

it does not bid me stay

smiles on me but makes no demands.

I sit by its fires

with the open sea at my back

my days here measured and finite.

This island is not my home

although it welcomes me.

At night I creep down to the shore

to dream of the growing boat

and the fading image of home

my arms curled loosely around this island

which welcomes me but does not claim me.

Grounded

They walk down this street—

perhaps from the bus

but I do not know this—

all I know is that

they walk down this street

a grocery bag hanging from

each arm, balanced white

ballast like double pendulums

keeping the beat.

Their legs between the bags

propel them forward but

the swinging bags keep them on the road.

They remind me of African women

with bundles balanced on their heads,

of Chinese peasants with

poles across their shoulders and

containers of water on each

extension.

The feet really do the work—

whether stirring the dust

or sucking through mud

or slapping the tarmac—

but the bags, the bundles, the buckets

keep them grounded

these kings and queens of the road.

Hickey's Mountain

I don't reckon I'll have me any more—

That time's over for me.

I birthed nine of 'em

three died right off, one's over to the school,

and, of course, there's this one here.

The others, well, they come by onct in a while.

I don't see them much.

Last night I had me a fine dream.

I was big—

big as Hichey's mountain over yonder.

Looked kinda like that ole mountain,

as a matter of fact.

But it was me all right

and I was buck naked

but I didn't feel no shame, no, none a'tall.

I was layin' out there, brazen as could be,

'n I spread my legs out wide's I could

'n tole all them chil'ren to get back

where they belong.

They come runnin' 'n skippin' 'n creepin'

'n crawled right up inside me.

They wiggled 'n curled 'n cuddled

until they was all cozy 'n quiet.

Then I put my legs together and lay real still—

still as Hickey's mountain over yonder.

My, it ware peaceful.

How Clever You Are

I see that you are well-prepared to survive
walking down a narrow shaded alley
your feet encased in sneakers
very nice sneakers that at one push
through the balls of your feet
will catapult you around the corner
faster than any assailant.
You carry a teddy bear for company,
a large safety pin firmly fastened to his stomach.
Yes, I will keep my distance
Yes, I know you are not lost, but hiding.
How well you hide
How clever you are.

Is that a box of cracker jacks in your pocket?
I am impressed with your quickness, your skill,
your control.

Yes, I will keep my distance
and thank you for letting me see you
I am impressed with how well-prepared
you are to survive.

Lessons of the Garden

Here in the South

I have learned the lesson of weed—

how weed can leap up, spread out, and obscure

the tiny flower I just planted,

choking it out as soon as I have turned my back.

I've learned how to hover over freshly-turned

earth with my thumb and forefinger poised

ready to catch the weed as it springs upward.

In the South, kudzu is the mother of all weeds.

The instructions for growing kudzu go like this:

"Stand in the middle of a paved lot. Throw one

kudzu seed as far as you can and run like

hell."

I am onto weed.

I have written the lesson of weed

in my book of relationships where I

relentlessly stalk and destroy all that

threatens.

But, I am in need of the lessons of a colder climate,

of Minnesota, perhaps.

I need to learn what happens when cold comes

    day after day until the ground is frozen and

    nothing can be planted.

Where only the trees and grasses and bushes with

    the deepest roots live to bloom, even briefly,

but oh, so lovely

Oh, so loved—for their survival in the harshest of climates.

Like the Ferris Wheel

like the ferris wheel

you

I would like to ride again

hoping that maybe

this time I won't

have to stop

in mid air

to get off

like the ferris wheel

you

I would like to ride again

hoping that maybe

this time I won't

throw up

like the ferris wheel

you

I would like to ride again

knowing that this time

I'm not as bound

to earth

lighter

I float more freely

like the ferris wheel

you

I would like to ride again

knowing that this time

wherever I go

I'll always

come round

to me.

Falling

falling

into your eyes

I know

      there is no other way

           to go

I make myself

a deep hole

through which you

can escape

if you wish to

Passing Through Chickamauga

It is indeed a momentous event

To be killed in war

And well could make one pause in awe

At what moves a man or woman toward death.

Easier to understand in the defeated old—

Some last gesture of meaning, some hope

That they will not have just lived.

But what have we told the young

That they would go so thoughtlessly to their end

In this field where the gentle cows graze?

How they must have stared, those brown-eyed ones,

At such sustained violence—blood running out

    to cool on the evening grass.

And though they turned their backs, surely they

    did not eat that day.

Lists

I make lists.
Usually each item is short, a mere clue and cue—

    cats

    tire

    Sandra

    mend—

When the items are very detailed—

    remember to turn the car port light out

      when you leave in the morning—
I know I am in trouble.

One day, when a very attractive woman was coming
to dinner, the list read—

    shop

    clean

    change cat litter

    wash salad stuff

    firewood

    bed—
I wasn't in a lot of trouble that day.

Made in the USA

When my grandmother was a child

everything she wore was local

very local not just Made in the USA

but made right there in Chilicothe, Missouri

flour sack underdrawers with four x's

across the bottom if the seamstress

was careful and dresses from chicken feed

sacks made deliberately with little pink

flowers on it (little blue sailboats for boys)

if the seamstress had good taste. Her shoes,

if she had any, probably came from Chicago

through the Sears catalog, but that would have
been

several children removed, so they were local too.

Socks, if she had any, mittens and sweaters,

would have been knitted from wool grown on

sheep within the county.

She was an all-American child, from top to bottom.

I am an international child, raised in a world

growing smaller every day. My shirt is from Sri

Lanka

shot through with golden threads. My jeans

were born in Chile, densely woven with

vaquero dreams. Shoes from the Philippines,

tropical white. The socks were grown and

loomed with my jacket in Guatemala with

all the colors of orchids. And even my bra is foreign,

from Brazil, perhaps inspected by one of

Hitler's descendants. But my underpants I

insist and always have insisted, are Made in the
USA.

If I have the accident my mother always prepared
me for

I will go to the hospital or the morgue where

everyone will know that although all my extremities

embrace international waters

at bottom, I am an all-American child

like my grandmother before me.

Mrs. Rogers' Eyes

Mrs. Rogers does not appear to be having a good day.

She stares at me as I approach

And in her soft, too soft, blue eyes

I see such bewilderment.

I imagine her scrolling through her mental rolodex,

her eyes fluttering to find the name that means me,

Hoping that with that name will come all the memories

      that define our relationship.

Her eyes do not sharpen and I know the

      rolodex is still spinning.

I lean toward her and whisper, "It's Sharon."

"Ah," she says, grabbing my hand.

"I'm so glad you came. I've been afraid to swallow."

"Ah," I say. "Ah, yes."

And we smile at each other.

Squirrel in the Road

We never have any luck. All we have is dumb perseverance. Let's face it. Most people who tried something four or five times would just give up and let it go. Not us. We know we're not normal. We just don't know any other way. You all know that squirrel—I think it's either the same one or at least a member of the same family—who runs halfway across the road, senses your car barreling down on him, turns to go back, then seems to say, "No. I was going the other way," and reverses direction to put himself directly in front of where you had swerved to avoid him in the first place? I have to confess I've killed quite a number of them, but you'd think their family members watching would learn something from the experience. You'd think they'd tell themselves and the little ones, "Keep going. Don't turn back." But no. And that's the way it is with us, but since we're human, there are so many more ways we can mess up. Our commutes take longer than anyone else's because we hit every red light and every stalled lane on the way home. We are often the cause of the stall even though we have our car checked out by the mechanic we've used for two generations. We wouldn't think of changing mechanics because that would be bad luck. Go figure. And we're the ones in the grocery story line whose bar codes are always scratched or obscured in some way, so it's "Price check on aisle four!" again and again. We've often gone to bed hungry because the store closed before they could sort us out.

Last year, my husband, Jeff, said to me, "Karen,

we've got to do something about our darned luck."

"I don't know what you're talking about, Jeff," I replied as I discarded the third can of soda whose pop-top had broken off in my hand. I began rummaging through a drawer looking for a hammer and a screwdriver.

"What I'm talking about is that today Mr. Price told me he's going to have to cut my salary another ten percent. That makes four cuts this year. At this rate, I'll be paying him in a few months." Jeff looked really distressed.

"But, Jeff, you know that's just the way our luck goes." I had found a voltage tester, but nothing that even resembled a hammer.

"Karen, did you ever think maybe we could change our luck?"

Well, that brought me to a stop right quick. I totally lost my concentration, dropped the shoe I was going to use to hammer the voltage tester into the soda can with, and gave him my full attention.

"Jeff, who have you been talking to?" I demanded. No one in my family had ever talked this way.

"Just try to have an open mind, Karen. Let me show you something." He had a kind of newsprint magazine in his hand. It was one of those freebies they give away on the street. Named *The Age of the Dawning* or something like that. Jeff moved Blackie, our three-legged cat off the table and laid the paper out. He opened it to a big ad.

UNLUCKY IN LOVE? CAN'T GET AHEAD IN YOUR JOB? DOES IT SEEM LIKE NOTHING EVER GOES RIGHT FOR YOU? screamed the headlines.

"Hm," I said. "Seems like they know us, doesn't it?"

"Just wait. Listen to this." Jeff was pretty excited, I'll tell you. He started telling me that this person, name of Guru Petunia, had a sure-fire program to turn your luck around. She couldn't tell it all in the paper because the program had to be custom-designed for you, but it had to do with crystals and tapes you listened to in the night while you were sleeping.

"And," declared Jeff, "The consultation, to see if it is right for us, is free. And if Guru Petunia takes us on, our luck is guaranteed to change for the better or we get all of our money back." Jeff was as excited as I'd ever seen him. I kind of worried that he was out in the middle of the road getting ready to turn around.

"How much money would this be that we'd be getting back?" I asked.

"Just a hundred dollars for the first level of transmutation," Jeff said too quickly.

"And then, after that works, we can decide to go to other levels."

He was looking at me wide-eyed and earnest, a look I had always found irresistibly charming. But today, I tried to plow right over the charm.

"And just how would you know all this if Guru Peculiar can't reveal it until the consultation?" I was fairly sure I knew the answer—my mother didn't raise no dummy—but I did like to see him work. My hands were on my hips and my face was fierce the way it was when I said "no" to the llama ranch even though the Anderson's on the TV infomercial were totally rich and relaxed on their ranch. Jeff and I knew exactly where we were, had been there many times before, and we'd play it out this time, too.

"Well, hon…uh…I was in the neighborhood anyway, and I just thought I'd pop in and see if she—it's Guru Petunia, by the way—could answer a couple of questions." Jeff was doing a great "ah, shucks" bit, his face so sweet we could have been rich if we could have bottled it.

"She was so kind, Karen. You've got to meet her. I felt like our luck was turning just from being in her presence. She had a sort of aura, you know. Said I had one, too, but mine was a bit tarnished, needed fine-tuning. She set me down and gave me a cup of tea—can we get some chamomile tea? I know you'd love it—and she just talked to me. I told her all about our bad luck, and she said the darnedest thing. You know what she said, honey?"

"No, Jeff. What did Guru Pecunious say to you before she took our hundred dollars?" My arms were now crossed over my chest and my eyes were as narrowed as they could be and me still be able to see.

"Oh, honey. Now, don't be that way. She really did say the most wonderful thing." Jeff's eyes took on a dreamy look and in his softest voice he said, "She said that all that bad luck *wasn't* our fault. He opened his eyes wide, grabbed my by the shoulders and looked right into me.

"She said it wasn't our fault, honey. Do you hear that? She said we could change it. And that's when I decided to go for it. You understand, don't you? Say yes, baby, say yes."

Well, when Jeff pours on the charm, the sincerity, *and* the sweet talk, I'm a goner.

I didn't believe Swami Pirogi had anything better than a mud pie in a rain storm for us, but right then, I gave it up. I wasn't going to douse his hope even if I didn't share it.

And as I said, "Okay, baby, tell me all about it," I felt something crack inside me, a kind of painless, almost audible crack, like a dry twig snapping in two.

Eager as a kid with a new magic kit, Jeff showed me everything. We had to make an altar near the center of the house. We decided the kitchen was the best place. He showed me how to set up the altar with three crystals in the center pointing out like a star and a candle just beyond each point. We had a green one for prosperity, a purple one for divine clarity, and a yellow one for hope and joy. Jeff assured me that all the paraphernalia had been blessed by what's her name. I'll say this for it. It was pretty. I don't think I could have gone along with bats' wings or dried spiders.

About this time, the kids came tromping in from

outside demanding their dinner, so we got busy opening up some cans of Chef Boyardee Ravioli and feeding everybody. Blackie enjoyed what our little one, Jamie, threw on the floor. After dinner, such as it was, the kids fled to their room to watch TV. The sound didn't work, but the kids were happy to supply all the dialogue and sound effects they thought were needed. I figured it was as good for their imaginations as anything else.

Jeff led me through the ritual we were to perform every night. First, we walked around the altar three times clockwise. That took a little figuring out since all our clocks were broken. Then, we had to read together out loud a special prayer for each candle as we lit it. When all the candles were lighted, we walked around the altar three times counter-clockwise, chanting "So be it" over and over.

Well, I was tired and told Jeff I was going to bed. Jeff was high as a kite on the energy he'd created doing the ritual and supposed he'd sit up a while with the boys doing sound effects for *Fear Factor*. The boys really admired his burps and thought his throwing-up sounds were the best. The boys excelled at screaming and Jamie screamed like a girl.

When I woke up to their screaming, I at first assumed they were still at it, but when I got up to go tell them to turn off the TV and go to bed, I found that smoke and flames were coming down the hall, and the boys and Jeff were screaming at me to climb out the window which I did in a hurry, stopping only to grab my purse. I joined them on the patchy lawn and we counted heads. Everyone was there. Jeff yelled over the crackle and pop of the fire, "Go move the car before it goes up. I'll get the hose."

I scooped up Jamie, told the other two to come with me, and ran around to the front. Blackie sat on top of the car grooming himself. Robbie grabbed him and we all got in the car. I got the keys out of my purse, only slightly amazed that they were actually there. When the car started on the first try, I was more amazed. Two pieces—no, three, counting Blackie—of good luck in one minute. It felt strange, but it also felt good, and I took a deep breath right into that place where the twig had snapped.

I drove the car about half a block, stopped, and sat in neutral. In the rear view window, I could see Jeff trying to untangle the hose that kept wrapping around his legs. He'd be okay, but the house was a goner.

I put the car in drive and drove out of the neighborhood and toward the highway.

"Where're we going, Mom?" yelled Robbie.

"Somewhere else," I replied.

"But what about Dad?"

"He'll be staying."

My Father Took Me Places

my father took me places

my mother couldn't be

bothered to go--

to small cafes run

by tired people

to bridges large

and small

through parks

worn from the feet of generations

to sit on concrete

benches dirty from

trees and birds

hard little grit pieces

scraping my thighs and

speckling my hands

to corner lots

to watch the boys

play basketball

and sometimes

to let him join in

for a bit while

I watched first

on one foot and

then on another

the sun turning my skin

wet through the dust that

settled over me stirred up by

the ball

and the pounding feet.

he never left me

alone for long.

he took me with

him places my

mother couldn't

be bothered to go

I was the witness

to his life.

My Father's Piece

Well, you know this stuff they say I'm hallucinating—they're a lot of them here—one big fat woman—big as June—and then a little one with a baby—sometimes her husband comes—they sit on the desk and pretend to work. You know, they'll hold a candle up and make like it's a phone. They just disappear through the window or wall if I go over there. Sometimes, when I get up in the night to go to the bathroom, the big one'll be sitting on top of the TV.

I think it's real strange that these persons—Phyllis calls them non-persons—I call them non-persons, too—I think it's strange that they think they can come here to lie down at night. They just start coming here around 12 or 1 and they leave around 6. There's a man with two little boys—cute little boys—they've got rubber bands and kerosene. After I go to sleep they roll up grass into balls and soak it in kerosene and drop it in my eyes or mouth. They're not bad boys, just mischievous. Their father just goes to sleep and lets them run loose. They'll all sit, perch, or lie on you. I have to move them to get up at night to go to the bathroom. Fortunately, they just annoy me—they used to scare me.

I don't know what they are. Sometimes I think they belong to another world—a spirit world your mother Phyllis doesn't see—my eyes, you know, are affected. Maybe they want to tell me something, but they won't talk. I ask them who they are, do they speak English—they won't answer me.

About this time of night, I can look out any window and see somebody I know—you, Maudie, Harold, Sandra. I tell your mother it's not polite to eat in front of you and not invite you in. She says it's OK, that you don't mind. But it doesn't seem right to me. I worry. I would like to invite you in.

Tomato Summer

She had planted them near the street. Not that she was totally happy to think of their picking up any of the car exhaust that might linger there, but because that spot, near the street, was the sunniest spot she had, and this year she wanted to give it to the tomatoes. She had moved three gardenia bushes that hadn't been doing too well anyway, and she left the half-dozen gladioli alone to struggle through or not. The gardenias did well in their new, less sunny spot; the glads burst out with their salmon-colored blooms while the tomato plants were still small.

She had spent seventy-nine cents each on three bushy little seedlings tagged "Better Boys." She had spent another dollar and nineteen cents each on two wire cages to support the plants. (She had one cage left over from last year's single planting of cherry tomatoes.) And finally, she invested five dollars and forty-nine cents in a bottle of fish-emulsion fertilizer so she could feed them organically. The fish emulsion was a murky brown liquid and did indeed smell like dead fish. She apparently wasn't the only one who thought so. Her big gray cat, Thomasina, was often found lounging on the mulch near the tomatoes in the days right after she fertilized them.

So, for under eleven dollars—one of her less costly projects—she now had three healthy, sprawling tomato bushes producing tomatoes so fast she had to pick five or six a day. She frequently weeded and adjusted the limbs in such small increments of ten or

74

fifteen minutes that it hardly felt like labor at all. Even with her attentiveness to them, several bold branches had escaped the cages and lay sprawling out into the nearby weeds. She left those weeds to be a cushion for the ground-tomatoes which she watched carefully for damage. As careful as she was, she had stepped on one stalk when she was moving around to feed them, but apparently she hadn't broken it because it continued to grow green and leafy.

She picked each tomato when it was about half red so as not to tempt the wildlife or the humans passing by. She was so greedy for them, handling them carefully, setting them in the deep kitchen window. Promising them that they would never go into the refrigerator where their taste would be altered, she ate them as they ripened, sometimes standing over the kitchen sink and letting the juice run down her chin. Their skins were tough and gathered up in her mouth like a wad of paper which she spit out. But the insides were all that she could have hoped for. They had the fire of the sun and the juiciness of the rivers in them. They fed the dryness in her and spoke to her of primeval wildness. She thought she would never tire of eating them.

She worried at night about the possible marauders in her little garden. Last year some animal had chosen to take one bite—just one!—out of each ripe fruit. That was another reason she approved of her decision to harvest them before they were fully ripe. She thought of the people who walked on her quiet street, particularly the ones who were out after dark.

How could they not be tempted to take just one or two tonight, and then perhaps emboldened by the ease and seduced by the taste, to return, perhaps with a bag, to take more the next night? She feared for her tomatoes, knowing how precious they were, and she tried to think of ways to guard them but could not come up with a plan that would work. Her greatest fear was of the children, the ones who had lived long enough to want what others had and to destroy what others had even if they didn't want it for themselves. She understood the child who might take just one, a bright, tender globe of taste and sustenance, for her mother. That child, she could almost forgive and indeed would give her one gladly should such a child politely ask. But the marauders she feared most were the vandals; they had none of her sympathy and no forgiveness.

She lay awake nights, sleeping in short bursts, and she rushed outside each morning to assess her treasures: to count them, admire them, stroke them, and pick the ones that were ready to come inside to the safety of her kitchen.

The tomato project was satisfying in every way. Even the broken sleep caused her to smile with satisfaction and anticipation. They were out there in the night, so close she could smell their leaves, spicy and soft, feel the firm green globes damp with dew, see them breathing in and out as they grew. Their limbs reached out in the night air, stretching to touch her. Again and again, through the night, she was able to lull herself back to sleep, caressed by and caressing her newest love. How sweetly with tomatoes she lay. Her greediness for them remained, but satisfaction nested in the same place like twins in the same womb.

Soon, more and more tomatoes were turning half red. The window ledge was full. She had lined them up from the ripest to the greenest so she could easily pick up the ripest and eat it, but now they were three deep on the wide ledge and four, no five, were fully ripened.

She had to do something quickly. It was not acceptable to waste any of her precious tomatoes, so she quickly ate two of them and was reaching for a third when she stopped herself. She had been so intent on eating them that she had neglected to taste them. Horrified by the blasphemy she had just committed, she quickly packed up the next six ripest fruits and took them to her gentle neighbors next door.

"I want you to have these," she said, offering the bag. "They are so delicious…and they've never been refrigerated." She wanted them to invite her to stay so she could watch them eat her treasures, but they didn't. Their thanks, however, was genuine, and she went home knowing that she had done the right thing, but she felt strangely sad and disappointed. Would they admire them, their color and firmness, their delicate scent? Would they eat them all or would they forget and leave one or two to rot?

That night, her dreams were troubled. She thought she heard her orphans, for that is what they had become, crying from next door. Their cries, some whimpering, some bawling, made her body ache for them and she rushed out into the night. Instead of lawn between her door and her neighbors' door, there was a thick wood. The streetlights were gone, and the darkness was warm and heavy. The woods fought her at every step as she pushed and stumbled through them. When she finally reached her neighbors' door, she flung her aching and breathless body against it, pounding it with both forearms.

"Let me in. I made a mistake. I have to have them back. They belong with me. They're mine." But her wailing and pounding were not answered. There were no lights in the house, and she could no longer hear the crying.

She woke up covered in sweat, her sheets tangled so tightly around her legs that she fell trying to get out of bed. When she finally freed herself, she rushed to the kitchen, grasped the edge of the sink with her hands, leaned toward the window ledge, and looked at the two rows of tomatoes. Only there were three rows. The six she had given away were back. Yes, she confirmed it. She recognized their shapes and sizes and shades of red as clearly as if they had names.

As she stared at them, a flood of joy began to displace the bewilderment, and she softened toward them, rocking a bit, welcoming them back, her sweet ones, her precious ones. The ripest one, the one on the far right, seemed to rock as if also nodding back at her.

It rocked harder and on the third swing toward her open face, it tumbled off the ledge and fell into the sink. The sound was of flesh splitting and the white sink was splattered with the red of sweet, ruined fruit. Before she could react, the next tomato and then the next began to rock, and soon they were all, one by one, throwing themselves into the sink, breaking open, and lying helpless as their juice slid toward the drain.

She plunged her hands into the mass of seeds and pulp and brought it up to her face, sucking, inhaling, taking in all she could. She did this over and over, but she could taste nothing.

When she awoke, the sun was high in the sky. Still in her nightgown, she went outside, put on her gardening gloves and began pulling up the tomato plants. She did not allow herself even to look at them as she stuffed them into large, black plastic bags and set them on the curb for the garbage men.

My Mother Is a Class 3 River

My mother is a class 3 river

an impatient tail-swinging river

flinging herself along the channel

designated for her

sweeping debris along

hastily gouging out the soft spots

on her banks

scouring the roots of trees

slamming into rocks

pushing stubbornly at logs

fallen in her way.

Without compassion

she insists on her way.

If you want to travel with her

you'll need a tough smooth skin

and a fast paddle.

Road Trip

The cars were still going by as they stood patiently on the side of the expressway. He was tall and slender with long blond hair reaching down his back. She was shorter and plumper. Her dark curly hair massed around her face making it look smaller than it actually was. They were a handsome couple, appearing to be in their late teens or early twenties. They stood quietly and erect, side by side and exactly parallel to the four lanes of traffic in front of them. He reached to the back of his head and pressed on a spot in the center.

"What are the parents saying?" Her voice was quiet and even, her lips scarcely moved, and she continued to look forward.

"Hush," he responded with the same calmness. "They're searching. They want us to turn up the visuals and orient one hundred degrees to the left." They executed the request in unison.

The cars were still going by. They were faster than the bodies watching them could be and larger, but the youths had been told to expect the unexpected and to await instruction.

"Now they want us to bend our right arms and extend them with our thumbs pointing up. Apparently that will signal the chosen one to stop for us." Again, they performed the action in unison.

"They have forms inside them like our forms. They look at us and wonder why we are here, but their fear keeps them going. We are waiting for the one with something stronger than fear of us." She continued to take in the feelings that flew past them. The blue one is too angry to even notice us. She has many tears in her head. That white one would hurt us if he could. The red one is holding a device up to her ear. She must be getting her instructions from the parents. We must remember to move our lips when we speak to them."

"The parents will remind us of all that we must do," he assured her. "All will be well….Look, the brown one is slowing down. Read them quickly now."

"There are two big ones like us in the front and a little one in the back. The big ones are exhausted and sad. They have been fighting each other without even knowing why. It is because of the little one. There is something very wrong with the little one's body, but he is excited to see us. He is calling us. His lips are not moving, but he made them stop and he is calling us to him. What do the parents say?"

"They say, get in quickly and go with them," he responded as he opened the rear door and pushed her in ahead of him. He jumped in and closed the door.

"Thanks a lot, folks. We've been waiting a long time for a ride. Hi, kid. How are you?" The little boy just grinned and climbed over her to sit between them. He leaned back on the seat, his legs straight out in front of him, a look of satisfaction on his pale face. The car pulled back into the stream of traffic.

"No problem. Where're you two headed? My name's Stan, by the way, and this is my wife Karen. That little charmer you're sitting with is Greg." The man's voice was too loud as he glanced at them through the rear view mirror. Karen turned toward them with a nervous smile.

"Y'all goin' far?" Her Southern drawl caught them by surprise, but he recovered quickly, rubbed the back of his head briefly and replied with exactly the same accent. "Jus' up the road a piece—to the truck stop in Baxington. Our aunt's pickin' us up there. My name's Dick, and this is my sister Jane."

Karen almost laughed. "Do y'all have a dog named Spot?"

They looked puzzled once again. This time, she replied, "No, ma'am. We haven't had that pleasure."

Karen and Stan glanced at each other covertly, as if agreeing that their passengers were a bit low on wattage. But that was all right with them. Not everyone had Ph.D.'s like them, and not half the ones who did had good sense. These two youngsters at least had good manners.

"Greg, shall we show them your favorite DVD?" Karen addressed the child in the back seat. He and the one called Jane were playing that hand game where one person makes a fist with a thumb sticking up and the other grabs it in their fist with their thumb sticking up, and so on.

"Yes, yes. You want to see it? It's *Aladdin*. You'll love it. Play it, Mom."

"Okay, baby. But first, where are our manners, son? You kids must be thirsty. Greg, show them where the juice is and you get one, too."

Greg scrambled forward to open a small cooler. He got out three small boxes of orange juice, handed one to the one called Jane and two to the one called

Dick. "Hold mine for me, will you?"

"Sure. Be glad to." Dick and Jane held their boxes.

"Here. Let me show you how they work. It's really neat." Greg took one from Dick, tore the straw off the side and inserted it into a hole. "See? Didn't I tell you it was neat?" Dick and Jane imitated his action successfully, and they all settled back in the seat as the movie came onto the DVD screen. Jane's hand rested lightly on Greg's leg and Dick held the orange juice, offering Greg sips at regular intervals.

In a few minutes when the movie was going strong, Karen leaned over and whispered to Stan, "Do you realize he hasn't complained of pain once since they got in?"

"I know," he replied with a laugh. "Do you think we could keep them?"

"If only," she sighed and with a smile, she leaned back in her seat and closed her eyes, her hand resting lightly on Stan's leg.

And so they continued rolling along on the expressway. Just as the credits to *Aladdin* were ending, Stan saw the Baxington Truck Stop. He pulled in and parked. "I guess this is your stop, kids." He looked in the back seat as Karen struggled to wake up. Greg lay stretched out on the back seat, asleep with his head pillowed on his arm. His rosy face had a faint smile on it and his chest rose and fell gently with each breath.

"What the hell? Where....?" Stan stammered helplessly. Karen quickly put her hand on his shoulder and held him.

"Don't ask," she said. "Don't ask."

The cars were still going by as they stood patiently on the side of the expressway. He was tall and slender with long blond hair reaching down his back. She was shorter and plumper.

Save Changes

I am neither then

nor now

I am one who

stands here talking to you

becoming.

we are not our past

though our past drags at us like empty calories

we are not our present

though something holds us here in consensual
experience

we are the schematic of our future

energy nets cast out to other realities—

what future will we choose?

The writing of this poem is already past

the time of reading this poem to you

is now but will be

gone in a moment

what of this will we keep for our future?

what will happen when

at the end of this poem

we press "close—save changes"?

Saving Grace

I look out of my window with surprise,

expecting nothing more than a quiet street,

a bush or two next to a river of concrete,

a place where nothing's born and nothing dies.

I look casually, just to rest my eyes

on something other than this close-held sheet,

never hoping to see a sight so sweet

it could have no other name than paradise.

Birds of rainbow plume flying low,

waterfalls flashing through the silky air,

flowers bursting from the ground like joy

shouting to the sun that gathers all below

and fills my weary eyes with sights so rare

I become the word no sad thought can destroy.

Ode to my Vibrator

Now I begin to understand

the celibacy of nun and widow.

Now I begin to understand

the peace in having a

dead or ascended lover.

If one is to be full of another,

at least the other can be quiet,

fixed, stable, a dependable object.

I never really worry if my vibrator

will change its mind, be unavailable,

feel neglected or withhold its pleasures.

I never worry that our relationship

will not last—nor do I send it flowers,

sweet notes or remember its

birthday. I trust it to be there

when I want it and to make no demands,

unlike this human, living love which

crowds my head, changes,

and demands that I, too, change.

on the occasion of our ninth anniversary

What places have we come from

that bring us here, to now?

Time-lapse photography running

superfastforward

would show blurs of movement.

My blur, flinging itself outward

from the center of this country,

rushing southward, then west,

shooting back and forth like a

pinball searching for points.

West, east, west, and east again—

north, Midwest, sketching out a

star of blurring flight and

finally zooming south again

to hover—with occasional darts

outward in all directions,

but hovering—circling around

this home we have made.

Your blur filling in an area so

densely, it almost seems

still were it not for the constant

shimmering and the quick

reachings out of flash.

Your traces packed the red Georgia

clay into a density you find

hard to escape.

Mine scarcely bent the grasses as

I passed.

Until we came

to this home we have made.

"Stretch, see the horizon, believe in

movement," I say to you.

"Be still," you reply. "Breathe deeply.

Come home."

Present and Willing

Sometimes all we can do is be present and willing

Sometimes we simply go

to the place where the sunset might be

to the page where the words might appear

to the person who might melt

to the mountain where the goddess might speak.

Present and willing; simply we go.

And, if the sunset is obscured by rain

if the page persists in its blankness

if the person does not choose to melt

if the goddess is mute

we have not wasted ourselves.

Present and willing

we simply go

we are there.

Rain

The early summer showers in Georgia

come suddenly and come hard.

Some are described as isolated

and some as scattered.

I have yet to understand the difference,

but those words never fail to elicit

my pity.

I see wandering tribes

of early humans separated in

the wilderness, scattered and

isolated,

looking for others of their kind.

Lost perhaps when a fall of

boulders

closed the end of their valley

leaving half at home tending and gathering

while others roamed the plains

hunting.

I see a musician with a melody

and a poet with words

yearning and calling for each other

but hearing no answer.

When I hear the tapping of the rain's arrival on

my metal roof, I run to the

center of the room and shout

out a welcome.

In the center of a room charged

with the fall of water

shaken loose to dance by

the deafening drumming,

I like to think that for a few moments

both the rain and I

are not scattered or isolated.

For a few moments we embrace

in the joyous reunion of what was lost.

Rare

At

first

a sperm

finds an egg

that welcomes

it and they join to

create a human child

a baby who grows into

the fullness of first its size

and then strength and finally

whatever intelligence it will have.

And, yes, if it's one of the rare ones,

this creature may develop a tiny piece of its

being into something we might

call wisdom

one   single

shining star

to top this

living tree

Resonance

Let me be the sustained

Sweep of cello

Resonating

Beneath your clear and

Separate notes

That move

Like the high leaves move

When pierced by

Shafts of summer's end

And let the hand

Lifted

From the music

Carry the shape of each note

The line of resonance.

Thanksgiving

The highway is littered with bodies.

Today, on the way to my mother's house,

I saw the bodies of

one chicken, five dogs, and two possums.

At each sighting, my stomach

heaved my heart

tensed and a sob

choked my throat.

When I arrived at my mother's

I saw on the kitchen counter--cold—

over ten hours dead

the body of a turkey

her guts piled beside her,

and my mouth watered.

The Breath

She took a deep breath and held it, trying to imagine what it might be like if this, indeed, were her very last breath. How would it feel when for the last time she felt cool air streaming through her dilated nostrils into whatever sacs held it, knowing that on the exhale, she could do one more thing, perform one more action in this world before the lights and sounds turned off?

She exhaled reluctantly when the pressure became too much, breathed normally for a while, and tried again. Her eyes fluttered, she sat up straighter, trying to make more room for the punishing air. Pressure built up in her head as the air fought to get out. Holding it hurt. Not sharply, but like a reverse blood-pressure cuff squeezing out, wanting release.

She knew that in reality, her last breath would probably not be a deep one like these she was practicing with—unless, of course, she was taken by the surprise of a gunshot or a car crash. Gasp, inhale, die. It could happen that way,but it probably wouldn't. More likely, over a period of time, the breaths would become infinitesimally more shallow. Just a hair's difference, the air sacs shrinking in capacity and power. Like the wrinkles on her face, the brown spots on the backs of her hands, the gray strands in her once honey-colored hair, change would creep, slower than grass growing, but just as surely.

But what, she wondered, as she took another deep breath, would it feel like to know this one was the last? Would it feel sweet, satisfied and savored, or would it feel desperate, anguished, and bitter? Should she, could she, pre-plan her last action, her last sound? Would she squeeze the hand that might be holding hers, or, if alone, would she smile and open her eyes wide? Would her last sound be "Noooooo" or would it be a grateful surrender of "Ahhhhh"?

Would she know everything she needed to know by then, either through accumulated reflection or perhaps by sudden insight? Would all the questions and contradictions her experience had generated suddenly fall into place the way a storm falls into a lake and smoothes out into a clear, still, reflecting surface over untold depths? Would she know all that she needed to know?

Why, she wondered, did it hurt so to hold the air in? Oh, she knew the physics of it. She had blown up, held, and played with enough balloons to understand the pressure. Had delighted in popping them and hearing the tiny explosion as the air rushed to get out. Had over and over again filled them almost to bursting, then released the neck and watched them fly around the room in a frenzy—of delight or panic? She wasn't sure, but she understood the physics and fully appreciated the energy in that release. She would like her last action to be as startling, as memorable, as a released balloon.

Nothing saddened her more than seeing a

dead balloon lying on the floor, its skin wrinkled and flaccid. If it's going to hurt, then the release should be spectacular. There should be something, some fireworks, some spiraling mad flight to show for all the pain, she thought, as she exhaled.

The Children of Atlanta

It isn't just that they were children

and died,

although that is enough

to make us gasp

with the fleeting knowledge

that death plays no favorites,

has no more purpose than a flying meteor.

It isn't just that they were black, male

and murdered,

although the rage of that fact satisfies before it

whimpers into complacent helplessness,

and we turn to our coffee

with a shake of our heads

blessing the luck that leaves us alive,

the wisdom that chose not to

make us young, black, male and dead.

The thought that hurts, that turns us aside

to lover, friend or other vice,

is that they died without comfort.

The hand that touched them

was not gentle—as they died—

No sound lullabyed

their bodies—as they changed—

No body breathed with them—

as they stopped.

The Eyes Have It

Sometimes when I get in my car

I consider not putting on the seat belt—

just for a few seconds

fighting the memory

that always comes

of your eyes

holding me

too precious

to waste.

I always thought it was your love

until now.

Now, I see your fear

and just as in your eyes

I first saw your love

and felt mine

now I see your fear

and feel mine.

The Lull

the chatter of the women

talking for each other

telling stories of the nearly

tragic made funny by

the nearliness of it.

we have escaped to spin

this story so it makes

us gasp at how close

we came to disaster

and laugh at how silly

we must have looked

as we survived—oh, you

had to be there to appreciate

the spin as we created yet

another family myth and

then a lull as we floated

on our laughter giving my

sister who was doubled over

with tears in her eyes

time to recover.

there must always be a

lull for our thoughts

our pleasure in this

kitchen event we are creating—oh,

you had to be there when

the lull reached its depth and

my mother grabbed up a

handful of the flesh hanging from her arm

and said right into the

heart of the lull

"my skin used to fit me."

The Movements of Your Dance (1)

If you would enter my room

In the softness you wear at night,

I might not know your gentleness

and, then again, I might.

For though you walk the day

in flippant phrase and cocky stance,

I know your body's inward step,

I know the movements of your dance.

The Movements of Your Dance (2)

The movements of your dance

Quicken me to silence

Like the river

Which flows downhill

Slowly

To its inevitable end.

Your body laughs into the shadows

And teaches the darkness

To breathe with you.

Catching light only to

Let it trail across your palm

And off your fingertips.

You and the moon and the sun

Three bodies sharing

The world's light

Quicken me to silence.

The Musicians

It is the last sullen dance

the band will play no more

they are tired—they work hard

on their finger bones

calluses grow like dimes

their cheeks stretched

by air and effort

they play this one last

dance the short version

but slow because they

are tired and because

they see in our eyes

that we are not

our finger bones are smooth-

tipped our cheeks fill

only with food and drink

and empty to form a

kiss, a promise that we

will send them home soon

where their hands will soften

to touch what they love almost as much

as their instruments

their cheeks will sag

against their teeth

tasting the tart and sweet

as they sleep their fingers

will twitch and their cheeks

will puff as they drift to

the last sullen dance.

The Nose Knows

You have spread the smell of me

around this room so thoroughly

that I encounter it at every turn

am forced to remember the me-ness

that you have squandered.

Had you no smell of your own

to leave?

How do you expect me to remember you

when at every turn

I encounter me?

The Note

(for Martha)

he said a note was

like a one-night stand

hit it and run

presumably

on to the next

encounter   not meaningless

but not to be

repeated

not to be savored

lingered over

dreamed upon.....

but   not meaningless

just a note

in a series that

might make a melody

or an excited run

toward that note

you might choose

to linger over

to savor and dream

upon   to caress

as if you had

finally found

the note you wanted

to love.

The Old Man and His Dog

I need to see the old man and his dog.

Every morning I sit

on my porch with coffee and journal

waking up and spilling out

on paper what the night

has dredged up for me to see.

A small apricot kitten

alternately provokes, distracts

and comforts me.

I sit with a full view of

my front yard laden

in summer with swamp hibiscus,

dahlias, daisies,

in winter still the

green promise of over.

As I write, the routines

go on about me.

To my left I hear the

little boys waking up

and yelling out their needs

in baby voices I do not try

to understand.

On my right the young beautiful

couple come out to trot behind

their Great Dane named for the

Roman conqueror Hannibal.

Across the street a woman I

have never seen before yells at

her dogs to shut up

and they proudly bark

back their love and understanding.

But I need to see the old man and his dog.

On the street before me

just beyond the flowers

that I grow for them,

people pass

on their way to something—

a bus, a friend, a store.

But the old man isn't going anywhere.

He walks slowly, watchfully,

in his right hand a simple

walking stick.

In his left a plastic bag

held by the handles

and a leash that leads

to a small black dog

who walks behind him

in the same measured tread,

head down, their footsteps

timed to adagio.

If he pauses to pick up trash,

which the bag suggests to me,

I never see it.

If he returns, and he must,

I never see it

never know if the bag is full.

I have not seen him for two weeks.

Although we have never spoken

and I do not know his name,

I have come to depend on

his passing.

I don't even think he knows

I exist.

But I have come to depend on

his passing,

And I need to see the old man

and his dog.

The Power of "Ms."

The phone rings: a woman's voice

"May I speak with Mrs. Sanders?"

"There's no Mrs. Sanders here," I reply.

"May I speak with Miss Sanders?"

"Sorry. There's no Miss Sanders here, either."

Hanging up the phone, I am satisfied that no

stranger trying to sell, solicit, or survey

has breached my privacy.

The phone rings: a familiar voice

"Ms. Sanders?"

"Yes," I reply, wary, but ever willing to play fair.

"Fuck you," she screams. "Just fuck you."

How wonderful, I think. How absolutely,

satisfyingly wonderful.

Now, we can talk,

Now.

We engage.

The People of the South

When the People of the South

hear that snow is coming

they don't believe it

but they crowd into stores

buying milk and bread

batteries and candles—

they haul in firewood

fill their cars with gas

check blankets

and wait.

The People of the South

do not believe

but they hope and they wait.

When the snow falls

and falls and keeps falling

the People of the South

open their eyes like large

round windows and into

the frosty air they breathe

a prayer that sounds like "ooh."

And as they walk through

the white streets all the People

of the South wave to each other—

a benediction of bright air.

The Pink and White Room

I woke from my sleep—

as innocent as a twelve-year-old

can be who has broken at

least four of the ten commandments.

I woke in the middle of the night

in the pink and white room

my mother had created for the

fantasy child she hoped I might

one day become. I knew what

her prayers were.

I could hear her muttering

the rosary of them;

I could see the words floating

through the air, residing in every

gift of pink and white,

dainty and sweet.

If only she believed enough.

I woke in the dark night

in the pink and white room

as much myself as I could be,

confused and startled

to see my father standing

in the doorway, fully dressed

back-lit like an angel from

the hallway light.

Silhouette of the other parent

saying, "Mr. Wyatt died tonight.

I have to go see the family. Do you want

to go with me?"

No, I thought.

"No," I said. "I want to sleep."

Years later, I know that

if I hadn't been in my mother's pink and white room

I would have gone with him

with all my heart.

The Putting On of the Bra

She bends over from the waist and lets

her breasts fall

into the cloth that will hold them

in just the right shape

at just the right height

to suit her station in life.

What does she think,

as with her hands, she

coaxes each breast to fit

into its appointed form?

Does she feel the softness made stiff?

Does she believe she is keeping them safe

until they are revealed

for a lover's delight?

How You Use Me

I am the wick in the candle

the hole in the do-nut

the space in the chair

I am the break in the bird song

the gap in the teeth

I am the held breath

the empty navel

the priest hole

the air in the bubble

I am the scar on the flesh

the white of the eye

the grooves on the handle

I am without meaning

until you use me

and I am continually

surprised

at how you use me

I am where leaves strain to go

the phantom step that jolts

the moment between ticks

I am totally free and therefore

useless until you use me

and I am continually

surprised

at how you use me.

In Between

Sometimes, when I turn my head

the world flashes off and then on again

So fast

So brief

I whip my head around to repeat,

confirm that break between now and then

but the break is sealed, seamless

the flash eludes and mocks me.

Like Alice--

I would like to be in the flash

in the flesh

Like Alice--

I would be changed

Like Alice--

I would be so grateful

to return intact

from the

"curiouser and curiouser."

The Rape of the Children Goes On and On

[*The refrain is from Yogananda*]

my lover pulls back

to look at me

and gently traces a

finger down those silken folds

my infant legs go limp

like rotten vegetables

as mother—flashlight

in hand, scowl on face—

says, "gotta see if you're clean

gotta clean this baby up."

> *Listen, listen, listen to my heart's song*
>
> *I will never forget you*
>
> *I will never forsake you.*

I am slicing zucchini

a friend is coming to dinner

slicing smoothly round thin slices

slicing for the pleasure of a friend

coming to dinner, the knife blade

sharp as it nicks my finger

and my father's voice yelling,

"you're just a fuck-up, that's all

you can't do anything right."

> *Listen, listen, listen to my heart's song*
>
> *I will never forget you*
>
> *I will never forsake you.*

"I love you," she says

"can't you just give me a

little more, a little more

time, a little more of you?"

"No, no more. We'll have to part,"

I reply clamping shut

all my openings as tight as muscles can

because his drunken breath

is whispering, "I love you, baby," and

his hand is between my legs.

> *Listen, listen, listen to my heart's song*
>
> *I will never forget you*
>
> *I will never forsake you.*

I walk into a party

the room is ringed with

small clusters of my friends

greeting each other

rubbing their words warmly

against each other

an occasional burst of laughter

enfolding the group

suddenly my hands are

clenched around wooden bars

as I stand in my crib

and watch my mother and brothers

playing and giggling on her big bed

and I do not know why I

cannot join them.

> *Listen, listen, listen to my heart's song*
>
> *I will never forget you*
>
> *I will never forsake you*
>
> *I will never forget you*
>
> *I will never forsake you.*

The Secret

It isn't that you don't know

it's just that I haven't spoken it.

To say I love you

is the scariest of all.

Just to know it

is scary enough.

Knowing also that I have

created you

out of the fire and water

my soul needs.

Knowing also that I create my own rejection.

Why do I feel that

"for my own good"

I must risk whatever

you will do with my confessions,

yield up my fantasies

and sit needy before you?

My face goes red

at the thought.

Can't you be my fantasy

just a while longer?

The Woman in the Moon

There's a woman in the moon.

She sits cross-legged

meditatively

mysteriously

turned away from us

her thoughts her own.

Last night I flung my leg up high

above the city lights and

goosed her with my big toe.

She dissolved in laughter

and sprinkled moon dust all over my belly.

Surely, something will come of this.

There: August 19, 1995

You told me you were going

to a party on Saturday night

and I thought it strange that you

offered no detail

offered no information

offered no invitation

but I didn't think too hard

about your reasons

didn't feel too left out

knew you had your reasons

and trusted them

trusted that

even if you

were going with someone else

even if you

were going where I was not welcome

even if you

were holding back something for you—

trusted.

And then Saturday morning

shuffling through my papers

to sort and do and throw away I found

an invitation to a party Saturday night

and I knew this was the one that

even if *you*

had not invited me

I was invited

I was a chosen guest

even if *you*

had not chosen me

even if *you*

did not expect me there.

A fantasy sprang up of

my going

even if you

did not expect me there

especially if you

did not expect me there

a fantasy you would not expect

a surprise on your half birthday

even if you

did not realize it was

your half birthday.

Details began to cluster

around the surprise.

I would wear a skirt

to show you that "yes, sometimes

I wear a skirt."

I would go to dance with you

to hold you on the dance floor

and I would tell you that

I had come to dance with you

even if you

did not expect me there.

And to kiss you

and to kiss you

and to kiss you.

I ate early

had a glass of wine

and by nine I was

dressed in my blue skirt

and soft white blouse

with sandalwood oil rubbed

into my neck.

The demons that came

to tear at my stomach

to tell me not to make a fool

of myself

to change my clothes

to change my mind

were small ones

and although they kept me

locked in my house

with fear that

even if you

saw me

you would not want me there

even if you

would not dance with me

even if you

would not let me kiss you.

I found my keys

left my house and drove

to the party where

even if you

were not there

even if you

did not expect me

even if you

did not want me

I was

there.

This Is For You,

This is for you, my lovely child,

With your scars and your pain

and your dark, dark skin.

Your rainbow names

all vowels and open

a mother's hope still clinging

to your growing limbs—

Natasha, Angel, Lakeshia, Shaniiii—

names without ends—

Sarita, Kendra, Marioooo…

Names that flash in your eyes—

Dia, Jeremiah, Syllllvia…

I feel your bodies singing.

Clothed like mortals

you know you are naked.

Give me smart mouth, sullen face,

indifference, contempt,

I am not hurt

I am not fooled

We both know that you are naked.

You are my future,

Not I, yours.

You are my best reason to die.

Let me feed you with my dying.

This is for you, my lovely child,

with your scars,

and your pain,

and your rainbow name—

Roosevelt, Deborah, Arie,

Michelle, Shirmary, Tiffany…

To Betray the Memories

You want to touch

I can feel it

and yet every time you touch

you remember

that other touch

that so electrified

your skin and soul.

Between your skin and soul

now, such memories loom

vibrant with longing and grief

that every other touch

disappoints, fails to penetrate

those memories, threatens

to leave you lonelier.

I would not ask you to

betray those memories,

but I will not touch

what I cannot touch

deeply

will not touch unless

I can go past the memories

that haunt you

will not touch unless

I am willing to betray the memories

that haunt me.

To Fleetwood Who Died on June 28, 1994

(Written on November 9, 1993)

How can I enter the world

of what it means for you to die?

You lie there looking at me

with soft eyes, eyes that are

looking dead ahead at the

inexpressible, the unspeakable.

You withdraw from me gradually,

not through lack of love.

How closely can I follow you?

Shall I let go of you or risk

letting go of life to follow?

I cannot keep you here.

You will not stay.

All my planning,

all my control, is not going to

keep you here.

You are part of

how I define my life and

I must change. I must change

in ways I cannot know,

cannot control,

cannot predict.

Thank you for the opening.

Thank you for the life you

shared with me.

Thank you for the death you

shared with me.

Thank you for the space,

the loneliness,

the quiet.

To Lose a Friend

We are a part
and I fear you
will never forgive
my saying so

I am a lone
and I fear you
do not care
to heal the wound

You are a way
and I fear you
will choose to travel
without me by your side

To lose a friend, a parent, an animal
companion to death
is pain in time with the comfort of when and how
and sometimes a bit of why

We turn to others living

and there is some consolation

some sharing of grief

some taking on of the lost one's beauty

To lose a friend

still living

not lost to others

who perhaps knew

how to make less demand

is a pain unspecific and endless

a grief unanswerable

a wound for which

there is no help in healing

a part gone

a lone left

a way lost

To Neil

I speak in praise of all things soft.

I did not go to your memorial service

but stood, instead, in the midst of acres

of new spring flowers—their pastel

shades rippling across my view.

I am not at your memorial service,

but in honor of you, I praise all things soft.

I praise the memory of your soft hand in mine,

of gentle brown eyes under a rippling sun,

of laughter that floats in the air and hovers near my ear.

I heap glory on things that yield—

cats asleep on deep plush cushions,

dog's damp noses and newly-turned earth,

candlelight and spaghetti,

whispered voices we lean toward to hear

and gentle smiles that say "no fear."

But, most of all, I praise soft bodies—

the pillowed shoulder, breast and thigh

that shapes itself around the hardness

of this world and lets us say goodbye.

Today Some of us

Today some of us killed

340 of our

children

and tomorrow

some of us will kill

more of our children

and because we have

developed such excellent and efficient devices of communicating heart-breaking news from anywhere in the world so swiftly that one atrocity follows another more quickly than we can breathe in and out

for each one

we have no time

to right our bodies

as they flail in the waves

lose their knowledge of which

way is down and which is up

our eyes wide with fear

we slam against wave after

unpredictable wave

knowing we must rise

or drown

Travelling

I have traveled by almost every means my culture
affords.

I have traveled by car plane bus train and truck

       horse donkey mule carriage cart and wagon

by buggy stroller piggyback knee-bounce

       and up-in-the-air-oops-a-daisy

by scooter tricycle bicycle motorcycle roller skates

       and skateboard

by elephant camel and big brown dog

by elevator escalator fork-lift sky-lift and tractor

by ferryboat yacht motorboat rowboat canoe kayak
water-skis

       rubber-raft and sailboat

by porch-swing tire-swing park-swing seesaw
rocking-horse

       and rocking chair

by balloon sled sleigh

       and once by llama

I have traveled by almost every means my culture
affords

and I still haven't reached home.

Violence in the Basement

As you speak of that large, admirable family

of white gloves and graciously-accepted civic
awards

your eyes cling to my face like tiny animals
scurrying

searching.

your broken limbs long since healed—

according to the x-rays—

break open again, dangle and weep

like shattered neon daisies.

As you speak of that family flowing across

the gentle hills like new snow in the quiet night

I hear the crashes of violence in the basement

the screams of small beings trapped by giant hands

the gasp of flowers crushed by giant teeth.

We both hold our breath to hear the whimper

that never left the basement

to hear it rising through the new snow to shatter

the quiet of the night.

We hold our breath to acknowledge

the violence in the basement.

Whose Mirror Is It, Anyhow?

I accept myself unconditionally right now

Right now I accept myself unconditionally

Unconditionally I accept right now myself

Unconditionally right now myself I accept

Myself right now I unconditionally accept

Myself right now I accept unconditionally

Right myself unconditionally now accept I

I now accept right myself unconditionally

Now unconditionally I right accept myself

Accept right my now self unconditionally I

Your Eyes

It may be a country song,

but I can't forget those eyes.

I look for them everywhere.

You knew good loving when you found it,

saw it walking toward you and opened

your eyes to let it in.

Your eyes taught me how to make a place

where butterflies blossomed

caverns of the past streamed with light

and the unicorn whinnied with delight.

I Am

I am

teasing the grace softly

and I will end with its gift

of laughter

and the wonder of silence.

With the wonder of silence

and its gift of grace

teasing the laughter

softly am I and

end I will.

Manufactured By: RR Donnelley
                     Breinigsville, PA USA
                     January, 2011